Facing Death with Hope

Living for What Lasts

David Powlison

New
Growth
Press
www.newgrowthpress.com

New Growth Press, Greensboro, NC 27404
Copyright © 2008 by Christian Counseling & Educational Foundation. All rights reserved. Published 2008

Cover Design: The DesignWorks Group, Nate Salciccioli and Jeff Miller, www.thedesignworksgroup.com

Typesetting: Robin Black, www.blackbirdcreative.biz

ISBN-10: 1-934885-52-5
ISBN-13: 978-1-934885-52-9

Library of Congress Cataloging-in-Publication Data

Powlison, David, 1953-
  Facing death with hope : living for what lasts / David Powlison.
      p. cm.
  Includes bibliographical references and index.
  ISBN 978-1-934885-52-9
  1. Death—Religious aspects—Christianity. 2. Future life—Christianity. I. Title.
  BT825.P69 2008
  236'.1—dc22

                                    2008011932

Printed in Canada
20 19 18 17 16 15 14 13   10 11 12 13 14

I s a life-threatening illness, a major life change, or just plain old age forcing you to face your own mortality? Is your eventual death looming like a dark cloud over your life? Are you sure of what will happen when you die? How are you dealing with your questions about death? Fear? Dread? Denial? Keeping busy?

Probably, like most of us, you'd rather not think or talk about your own death. But ignoring your death won't stop it from happening—the mortality rate is still 100%. Medical advances extend lives, but no one lives forever. In the end, doctors lose every patient. Eventually you and everyone you love will die. Every life on this earth ends in death.

But is our death really the very last sentence in our book of life? Or is there something beyond death? Christians have testified with all their hearts for centuries: "I believe in the resurrection of the dead." What does that mean? It means that if you follow Jesus, your physical death will not be the last sentence in your book of life. Jesus' resurrection makes death the second-to-last sentence in your life. When you die, if you believe in Jesus, you will hear his final say on your life: "Well done, good and faithful servant!…Come and share your master's happiness!" (Matthew 25:21).

Perhaps you know that Jesus rose from the dead, yet when you think of your death you're still full of fear and dread. That's because just knowing the facts of Jesus' life, death, and resurrection is not enough. You must know Jesus intimately. The courage to face your death comes as you put all your faith and trust in him. This booklet is written to help you face death honestly and know Jesus intimately.

Death Is Not a Friend

When people finally muster up the courage to talk about death, they often romanticize it. They talk vaguely about release from pain, going to a "better place," and being reunited with loved ones. But the Bible never portrays death as a friend. Death is called "the last enemy." Death is the final and ultimate loss. It feels unnatural and wrong because it is unnatural and wrong. We were created by God to live forever. Death is not what God intended for his world.

Facing the Shadows of Death

You don't face death just once at the end of your life. Throughout your life you face what David, in Psalm 23, called "the shadow of death" (v. 4). A shadow brings the looming sense that the dark is approaching. Walking through the "valley of the shadow of death" takes many different forms. Death is the ultimate loss, but many smaller losses also bring the shadow of death into your life. You have probably already faced some of these shadows:

1. *Loss of health*: Whether you are struggling with a chronic illness or a sudden catastrophic event, the losses that come with physical suffering foreshadow death.

2. *Loss of loved ones:* When death comes to those we love, we feel the shadow of death keenly. But we also experience loss when a relationship ends for any reason. When you experience betrayal in a relationship, you are getting a small, bitter taste of the alienation, isolation, and abandonment that is the ultimate experience of death.

3. *Loss of youth:* The years pile up, the hair turns white, the wrinkles form, the body starts to break down, and the memory starts to fail. It's as though fingers of darkness are reaching out to you.

4. *Loss of independence:* As you age, you experience weakness in various forms. Old age can make you as helpless as a young child, but for children the

expectation is of gain. As you age your expectation is only of loss.

5. *Loss of usefulness:* If you live long enough, you will outlive your usefulness in the workplace and watch life go on without you.

6. *Loss of meaning:* As you get older, possessions, others' opinions, status, success, and whatever else you were striving for will lose their significance.

These losses can shadow your life at any time. Whether you are young or old, every significant suffering, loss, and evil you experience leaves the bitter taste of death in your mouth.

The Cause of Death

Why are there "shadows of death"? What brought all this sorrow and sadness into the world? What causes death?

When we talk about why someone died, we usually talk about the immediate reason that they died—accident, old age, illness, a natural disaster. But the Bible deepens our thinking about the cause of death. Paul said in his letter to the Romans that "the wages of sin is death" (Romans 6:23). Sin is living in God's world and acting as if we are in charge. Adam and Eve were the first people to act like their own gods and disobey the one true God, but each of us has followed in their footsteps. Death is the sad result. The fear and dread we feel when we face our own death stems from our deep-down sense that we have failed to perfectly obey God. We deserve to die.

But who tempted Adam and Eve to live as if they were in charge of the world? Who tempts us? Satan. So, at a deeper level, he is the cause of death. The Evil One is called the murderer from the beginning. The Bible describes those who are held in bondage to the fear of death, as being enslaved by the devil. He is a killer (Hebrews 2:14–15).

At the deepest level, God's holy and just wrath means death. Every cause of death—hurricanes, old age, cancer, the wages of sin, the murderous power of Satan—is a subset of the holy and just wrath of God on sinners. We are all touched by the curse, and the curse gets the last say on our earthly life.

Jesus Faced Death for You

But for those who know Jesus, death doesn't have the last say, it has the next-to-last say. The last word for the Christian is the resurrection. The last word is life. The last word is mercy. The last word is that God will take us to be with him forever. God's free gift of eternal life stands in stark contrast to "the wages of sin is death" (Romans 6:23). Jesus stands in contrast to the killer, the murderer, the slayer. He, the only innocent person who ever lived, faced death not for his own sins, but for the sins of his people (John 3:16). Jesus faced death for you.

On the cross he faced death in all of its dimensions. He was killed by asphyxiation and torture, but this was only the physical cause of his death. As he died he bore the wages of sin, suffered the malice of the evil one, and experienced the holy wrath of God. He, the innocent one, willingly died for the guilty.

When he freely gave up his life, death was slain by God and Jesus rose to new life. God's grace destroyed the destroyer and death was thrown into hell. Because of Jesus life has the last say. Because of Jesus you don't have to experience death as he did. He has already paid for your sins. You will die physically, but rise to life eternal (John 3:16).

How Can You Be Sure That Eternal Life Is Yours?

Come to Jesus, ask for forgiveness for your many sins, and believe that his death paid the price for your sins and his resurrection is your guarantee that you also will live forever. This is Jesus' promise to you: "I tell you the truth, whoever hears my word and believes him who sent me has eternal life and will not be condemned; he has crossed over from death to life" (John 5:24). Because of Jesus you don't have to fear that when you die you will experience God's judgment. Jesus has already experienced that for you. What is waiting for you after death is real life—eternal life. You don't have to earn this life. It is God's gift to those who put their trust in Jesus. This is how the apostle Paul explains it: "For the wages of sin is death, but the gift of God is eternal life in Christ Jesus our Lord" (Romans 6:23). We all deserve death, but Jesus died in our place. When you trust in him, you no longer have to fear death, because now you share in Jesus' life.

The eternal life Jesus gives is life the way it was meant to be—free from evil, sorrow, and sadness, and rich in everlasting joy, peace, and purity. The natural, well-earned wages of human life bring death and grief, but God's mercy and grace bring the delights that are at his right hand forever.

Sharing in Jesus' life is how you face all the shadows of death in this unhappy, fallen world and how you face the final darkness of death itself. Because he is alive, you know he will be with you when you die. Because he is alive, you know he will be waiting for you after you die. Because he lives, so do you.

Jesus Faces Death with You

Isolation comes with all suffering, but it is even more pronounced when you face death. As you face death, the proverb, "The heart knows its own bitterness" (Proverbs 14:10, esv) becomes very real. No one on earth will go through that door with you. But remember David's words: "Even though I walk through the valley of the shadow of death, I will fear no evil, for you are with me" (Psalm 23:4). Who is with you? Jesus is with you. He says, "I am with you always" (Matthew 28:20).

Your friends and relatives cannot go with you as you die, but the one who is closer than a brother promises to never leave you nor forsake you. Jesus has a firsthand knowledge of what you are facing. He will be with you as you face death and as you die. His life, death, and resurrection are your guarantee that beyond death's door is a glorious new life. This is the reality of your faith. Your faith is not a nice theory or a bunch of sweet, comforting, religious platitudes. God himself will be with you in the moment when death stretches its fingers toward you.

Face Death Like Jesus Did

Because Jesus is with you, you can face death as he did. How did he face death? Was he calm and unaffected? No, he experienced death as a terrible enemy. On the cross he cried out words from Psalm 22: "My God, my God, why have you forsaken me?" (Psalm 22:1; Matthew 27:46). Jesus lived out this psalm of death and torture on the cross. But this is also a psalm of hope: "For he has not despised or disdained the suffering of the afflicted one; he has not hidden his face from him but has listened to his cry for help" (Psalm 22:24). Jesus' cry of desolation and forsakenness was in the light of his certain hope that God does not finally forsake those who are afflicted.

Jesus was not a stoic as he died. He looked death right in the eye, felt keenly its pain, degradation, horror, and loss, and then trusted his heavenly Father as he said, "Into your hands I commit my spirit" (Psalm 31:5; Luke 23:46). These words are not calm, cool, and collected. They are the words of a man who is fully engaged with his troubles, fully engaged with his God, and bringing the two together in honest neediness and honest gratitude. The two sides of faith—the need and the joy—are both present in Jesus' experience.

This Jesus is with you. This Jesus is alive and able to help you face death with faith. You can draw near to him. He will give you forgiveness, mercy, and help in your time of need. He endured, "for the joy set before him" (Hebrews 12:2). He will be with you, so you also can endure. You don't have to shrink back and pretend you're not going to die. You don't have to pretend it doesn't hurt. You can entrust your soul to your heavenly Father just as Jesus did.

Jesus Is Waiting for You

A friend of mine often asks people, "Who are you looking forward to meeting when you get to heaven?" People tell him about their loved ones, or interesting people from the Bible, but almost no one says, "Jesus."

Many years ago in *Time Magazine* there was an article about people who were facing death. Hundreds of terminally ill people were interviewed and photographed. Most of their pictures looked dreary and sad. But an elderly man's picture almost jumped off the page. His face was full of life and vitality. In his interview, he said he couldn't wait to see Jesus. He was joyful in the face of death because he was looking forward to seeing his Savior.

You cannot face death with true, honest courage unless you are looking forward to meeting Jesus—the one who faced death for you and is now alive and with you. Are you looking forward to meeting the Lamb of God who took away your sins? Do you long to hear your Good Shepherd call you by name? Are you looking forward to going to your heavenly Father's home? It's a home of glory, filled with the radiance of the Holy Spirit. In God's home all wrongs are made right, all darkness becomes bright, all losses are restored, and all tears are wiped away.

When you pass through death, you will pass through to the moment when faith becomes sight, when you will actually see the one whom you love sight unseen. To die in the hope that God is with you is to pass through the loss of all things into the gain of all things, into the gain of Christ.

Practical Strategies for Change

Practice Dying, Practice Living

You can start to prepare yourself for your death right now. Begin by asking yourself, "What am I living for?" Are you living for what will last forever? Or for what will die with you? My wife likes to collect stones from all over the world, so our house is full of stones. Stones last. We also buy milk every week and, even when it's kept cold, milk doesn't last. What are you collecting? Stones or milk?

You came into the world with nothing, and you'll leave the world with nothing. You can't take your successes, your achievements, your possessions, your spouse, your children, your grandchildren, and your friends with you. These are God's good gifts to you. But if you are living for the gifts, not the Giver of gifts, you will find that when you die all you have lived for will perish with you—it will all be sour milk. There's a proverb that says, "When a wicked man dies, his hope perishes; all he expected from his power comes to nothing" (Proverbs 11:7). The "wicked man" isn't necessarily an axe murderer or a pedophile. He is simply someone who has put his hope in the perishable. So he is living as if there were no God, no wrath of God on sin, no Christ who saved us, and no day of judgment.

John Newton called all the perishable things we put our hope in "schemes of earthly joy." We feel the shadow of death on us when we experience the loss of our earthly joys. But it is God's mercy to let us see, before we die, that all of our earthly joys are perishable, just like milk.

Remembering this will help you face the shadows of death fruitfully. As you practice dying to your "schemes of earthly joy," you are actually practicing the art of living. Learning the art of dying well in a fallen world means you are also learning the art of living well. Facing the many smaller losses in your life means you are dying many small deaths each day, month, and year. Jesus spoke of this way of life to his disciples when he said, "If anyone would come after me, he must deny himself and take up his cross daily and follow me" (Luke 9:23).

When you experience hardship and grapple with the death of your dreams, hopes, and desires, you will find out that only love for God and others is imperishable. This will prepare you to face your last enemy, death. Because you have faced all the little enemies, all the scouting parties, all the raiders from darkness in a way that is fruitful, when you come to the moment of your death, you will be able to say with David, "Though I walk through the valley of the shadow of death, I will fear no evil" (Psalm 23:4).

Accept the Reality of Your Death

As you practice the art of living well, you must also accept the reality of your death. This sounds obvious, but in our world people work hard at *not* facing their eventual and certain death. If you are to walk through the valley of the shadow of death and fear no evil, you must look straight at the shadows of approaching death. The Bible's description of life, death, suffering, hardship, hope, faith, need, and outcry is so graphic because God wants you to face what is happening, to look at it, and to talk about it with those around you.

If you are facing death in a hospital bed, talk with the nurse and say, "You know, I am going to die." Talk with your visitors and say, "You know, I am going to die."

Most likely they won't know how to handle your talking about your death. They might respond as if you had just said an obscenity. Or they might say, "Oh, no, no. Everything is going to be fine. We have the best doctors here."

You may even have to say to your pastor, "I am going to die." Saying this out loud doesn't make you a pessimist, and it doesn't mean you won't be thankful if your life is prolonged. You are going to die, and you ought to talk about it honestly. But you can talk about it honestly only if you face Christ.

Face Christ

You face Christ. You face death. You face Christ. You look at death, and you look through death—beyond the shadow of death to the light that dawns after the darkness. If you are facing the living God, the Lord of life and the giver of all mercies, you have every reason to look death straight in the eye. You're able to look past death toward something that is good, lasting, and wonderful. When you look past death with the eyes of faith, you will see a river of delight in the presence of the Lord himself; you will see yourself feasting at his table and drinking from the fountain of life (Psalm 36:7–9).

Meditate on Psalm 71

To help you face your death and face Christ, meditate on Psalm 71. It reveals the same truths as Psalm 23, but from the perspective of an elderly person. He is old and gray, his strength is failing, but three things are still true about him:

1. *He has faith.* God is still his refuge, rock, and fortress. He pleads with God to not forsake him in his old age saying, "Do not cast me away when I am old; do not forsake me when my strength is gone" (v. 9). He honestly faces the fragility of life and puts his faith in God and the resurrection. He says, "Though you have made me see troubles, many and bitter, you will restore my life again; from the depths of the earth you will again bring me up" (v. 20). His many troubles have not destroyed his faith. Instead, they have made him even more dependent upon and confident in God.

2. *He has joy.* Because he knows where he's going, he has a reservoir of fundamental, honest joy. You cannot pretend when you are facing death. Either you're anchored in the certainty of the resurrection and full of joy, or you're not anchored and full of

fear. Because he is full of Christian joy, he can say, as he faces death and struggles with aging, "I will ever praise you....My mouth is filled with your praise....But as for me, I will always have hope; I will praise you more and more....I will praise you with the harp...I will sing praises to you with the lyre....My lips will shout for joy when I sing praises to you" (vv. 6, 8, 14, 22–23).

3. *He has love.* Faith expresses itself in love. Love for God is always expressed in love for others. The psalmist says to the Lord, "Since my youth, O God, you have taught me, and to this day I declare your marvelous deeds. Even when I am old and gray, do not forsake me, O God, till I declare your power to the next generation, your might to all who are to come" (vv. 17–18). He has a sense of legacy; he's proclaiming to those he loves that he is dying in hope. You also are called to love others by leaving them a legacy of hope. It doesn't matter how you do it—a death-bed prayer, a letter written to a grandchild, a call to a straying friend, a chat with your nurses— but you are called to declare to the next generation of the living that you are dying in hope.

Your love for others might also express itself in making amends to those you have hurt. Are there people in your life you need to forgive? Are there those you need to ask forgiveness from? Love doesn't wait or stand on ceremony; it takes the lowest place and goes in humility to others.

There is nothing more powerful as you face death than faith, joy, and love. They keep you from turning inward. By faith you look right through death to the one who is your anchor. As you look at Jesus, the anchor of your soul, you will be full of joy. And your faith and joy will overflow in love to others. You will be able to imitate Jesus and reach out in love during the final days, hours, and minutes of your life. Because your Lord is with you, your faith and love will operate right up to the end of your life.

Like many of you reading this, I have faced death. In the fall of 2000, I needed open-heart surgery. I was diagnosed on a Friday and surgery was scheduled for Monday, so I had a weekend to face the possibility of my death. In the wonderful mercy of God, my faith did not fail. The Lord who saved me continued to save me, and that weekend was one of the most wonderful weekends of my entire life. Every lesser distraction fell away, and all that was left was love for God and people. It was a rich, fruitful weekend of love. I remember heading into the anesthesia and this was my final thought:

I will wake up one way or the other. I could wake up in no pain, in the presence of Jesus Christ whom I love, and see him face to face in the land of the living forever. My race will have been run, and the eternal kingdom will have begun. Or I will wake up and feel tons of pain. If I wake up in this world, I will also be in the love of God, but by faith, not by sight. And I will wake up to a life that will have purpose and meaning to the very end.

This is how, by God's grace, we face death; this is how, by God's grace, we live life.